TREMOLO

TREMOLO

poems by

Alice Derry

RED HEN PRESS | *Pasadena, CA*

Book design and layout by Ina Jungmann

Library of Congress Cataloging-in-Publication Data

Derry, Alice, 1947–
  Tremolo : poems / by Alice Derry.—1st ed.
    p. cm.
  Includes bibliographical references and index.
  ISBN 978-1-59709-232-6 (alk. paper)
  I. Title.
  PS3554.E75T74 2012
  811'.54—dc23
                          2012005556

The Los Angeles County Arts Commission, the National Endowment for the Arts,
the Ahmanson Foundation, the Los Angeles Department of Cultural Affairs, and the
James Irvine Foundation partially support Red Hen Press. Creation of this work was
made possible in part by the Artist Trust Grants for Artist Projects (GAP) Program.

First Edition
Published by Red Hen Press
www.redhen.org

Acknowledgments

Many thanks to the periodicals and anthologies in which some of these poems originally appeared in earlier forms:

A Fierce Brightness, Twenty-Five Years of Women's Poetry (anthology): "Anne"; *Calyx*: "Anne"; *Crab Creek Review*: "Tremolo," "On the Radio, Mozart's Piano Trio #7 in G Major," "I Mean Beach, Fir, Yellow"; *Crosscurrents of the Washington Humanities Association*: "You, Teacher," "The Planet Closest to Us," "Praise," "Visiting the Elgin Marbles," "Solstice"; *Fine Madness*: "Beech"; *Floating Bridge Review*: "Beech" (reprinted), "Visiting the Elgin Marbles" (reprinted); *Hubbub*: "Waking, Walking, Singing in the Next Dimension" (winner of the Adrienne Lew Award for volume 20), "Elephant Rides"; *Interdisciplinary Humanities*: "Precarious," "His Own," "Crossing Puget Sound," "Praise"; *Jump Start* (anthology): "Hardhack in Bloom"; *Long Journey* (anthology): "Precarious"; *Oregon Literary Review*: "But This Distance"; *Poetry East*: "Nootka," "Wings"; *Poetry.us.com*: "Although I Laid Carnations," "Nootka" (reprinted), "Anne" (reprinted); *Skagit River Anthology*: "Gerüche," "What My Student Discovers"; *Willow Springs*: "Deposition," "For Morris Graves from a Novitiate"; *Windfall*: "Finding the Poem."

My deepest gratitude to Charlotte Warren, who guided these poems to completion and whose patience was unbounded; to Tess Gallagher, for her devoted, unstinting, and comprehensive attention to the manuscript; to Lisel Mueller, whose careful listening has enriched my work through thirty years. I thank Jesse and many colleagues and friends—you know who you are—for support and love of the poems. A summer writing grant from Peninsula College gave time to help complete this manuscript.

for Bruce and Lisel,
loving you and being loved

This shaking keeps me steady. I should know.

Theodore Roethke

Table of Contents

V: Turn

TREMOLO

I: Klingen

from German: to sound, to resonate

like handkerchiefs waving on a railway platform when
one is leaving everything one loves
—Marcel Schneider on Chopin's Mazurkas

Although I Laid Carnations

1.
I wasn't there
to wash my mother's body.

The day before, yes.

When the home nurse came,
we cleaned her together, rolling her gently
on her side so we could wipe away the feces,
rolling her back to lift the too-heavy breasts,
dry the gathered sweat.

And each time we touched, each time
we moved her, she cried,
No. No. No. Although she could hardly speak.
Had said her goodbyes two days before,
making me listen.

After his call, by the time I could get to her
—three hours away—my brother had already
washed her and dressed her again
in the flimsy hospital gown.

But nothing in it of ceremony,
although I laid carnations
to frame her face and cover her crossed hands,

thinking of Hamlet's mother and Ophelia,
sweets to the sweet, thinking not even
of the real, but of some other sore heart's imaginings
to help me.

2.
Walking into work
in the early quiet
where a few minutes alone
is all I'll get today,

I can try to imagine
the Iraqi Shiite woman
the radio has brought me.
She is the one who keeps the dark stone house
for the ceremonial washing
of the Shiite dead.
She didn't elect this work.

Twenty-two when I saw the first body.
I said to myself, your four children
will starve if you don't do this.

The reporter describes how she
begins by covering the genitals
with a small square of white cloth.
Onto the scalp, she touches a circle of soap,
which widens to foam. The rinsed hair
returns to ringlets. With the *loofah* sponge,
she scrubs the body until it emerges, burnished,
ready to be wrapped in white linen for burial.

If pressed, she will tell you
she has never gotten used to it:
what was hardest, the woman they brought

to her, burned all over—
clutching her baby so tightly,
they had to be washed together.

3.
When friends ask, this first year
my daughter's gone from home—
*Don't you wish she was always
a child, holding to you?*

No, I say. *No.*
No. I want us
to be able to let go,

one body, then two.
From the tight embrace of the first years,
a child gathers herself
to walk away.

The air remains.

This Shiite woman has given me
a part of herself, her gift,
as I stumble out of my car
in the half light of spring,
all the birds back
to help us hear air.

Transubstantiation.
One thing becomes another.
Mere thought leads to the touchable child.

As she feeds her children the evening meal,
the woman who washes bodies knows well
what flesh is made of
how necessary the solid body is,
which becomes earth, its sure path.

When her children crawl into her lap at bedtime,
that's a different matter.

WHAT MY STUDENT DISCOVERS

on our visit to Europe, 2007

She chooses to visit the cemetery
of this little Austrian town on the Danube.
Could 2,000 have been sent to the camps
just from here? she asks when our class
reassembles, describing the holocaust memorial
set among trees. *On other graves,* she adds,
you could see the swastikas.

Graves of the men, teenaged boys really,
who fell invading Russia in '41—*Wehrmacht.*
They had trudged across the wide stretches
of ripening wheat, deeper and deeper
into a summer, which like all heat and fruitfulness,
promised to be forever.

Both of us mothers, my student and I stand
in the same late summer sun. Other people's children
are moving across Iraq's sandy fields,
into the villages, through the neighborhoods,
which were once ancient Mesopotamia.

I'm trying to help her understand—
these Austrian sons lifted up each comrade
gunned down. They sent the bodies home
to cemeteries like this one.

The living soldiers struggled on
toward Stalingrad, leaving behind them—
in ditches they covered over
after they had done the shooting
and the bodies had tumbled in—
the Jews of Russia.

SOLSTICE

talking to my daughter

1.
In the small indigo clarity before dawn,
the new moon cradles the old moon in its arms.
Around them, a wheel of ice.

Once the gray comes, you and I are out
where frost has coated every grass blade, tramping about,
our jackets too scanty, or some other mild treachery,
seeing, if only as irony, how the beauty
holds still under each sharp
intake of breath.

2.
On the radio a man tells of recording the sounds of our earth,
its *suspiration* so slow he had to speed up his audio.
Then like the whales calling and surging,
surf thumps against a thousand beaches
and we hear the constant earthquakes of the wrinkled mantle
settling, shifting.

As in sleep we turn to keep our bodies afloat
these long nights—not to succumb.

3.
I suppose early darkness gives our friend Warren,
over eighty, permission to reach back fifty years
and bring us his time in Germany as a soldier,

connection being what he had to do,
keep track of the field units and who was where.
So often he says, you'd reach out,

and it was silence, *you'd lost that group,*
and the damn tanks, if they crossed over the fragile
communication line spread on the snowy ground, just one
pulsing artery to keep things together, the wire would sever.

The shooting over, his company occupied the central hill country.
He had time, took the trouble to get a three-day pass,
take along a buddy to visit a cathedral.
He knew he was in a great place.
Was the rose window even there, or was its glass
hidden in the cellar? he asks us,
staring into an interior only he can see.

That winter in the Harz, his company lived
in wood and earthen shacks, like caves,
never warm, a whole winter never warm, but alive
in the terrible cold of '44, the German nation around them,
quiet and starving.

4.
Two people who love each other, mother and daughter,
realize in their short holiday
that the rest of their lives together is separation,
which includes reunion with its high-pitched happiness,
tedium flaring as temper,
but not routine's settled rhythm—
small niches, how tea with each other
or the daily walk up the hill

mimic, in the best way we know,
the safety we've let ourselves believe.

But This Distance

Bruce reaches his hand, swollen from climbing,
helps me up one spruce root
to the next, then coaches me softly
down the headland banks hung only with rope.
At the creek ford, our daughter balances his pack
across the mossed rocks.

Once we've landed on safe Pacific sand,
we make our camp, something we all know
how to do. That's when the bright arguments sear
like sudden August heat dissolving fog,
and we bruise flesh with words.

What could contain it but this distance,
pulling us southward on the narrow strip
pressed between rainforest's labyrinth
and an ocean world we might have come from
but can no longer enter—each low tide
revealing rocks shiny with seaweed and barnacles?

"Camping's not free," Bruce reminds us.
A thin slip of high-tech nylon
is shelter. What we've carried,
all we have to eat and where we go,
our legs must be equal to.

Next morning, we climb another headland,
drop down on a cove buried in fog.
Nothing to do but sprawl along a spruce skeleton,
eat our lunch, wearing out old jokes
until the sun breaks through.

These stolen days are lived by the tide's allowance.
The yield's a small pile of sea glass,
the purple-rayed book of an open clam shell.
Last light sheens the crescent of ebb-tide breakers,
then the Milky Way crowds down.
Around the fire, stories
of our past camping disasters—
mosquitoes, rain, dust. How we persisted.

Dark is dark and the heap of low coals
unravels to ashes.
Without light we're afraid,
let the tent's small shelter hold us close.

Sometimes they show themselves,
those who know how to live here—
crows and seagulls, osprey, a pair of ravens.
A snake suns itself each afternoon
by the log we staked out as table.

And when we've used our allotted time—
home across the last steep headland, our daughter
far ahead and glad to be free of us
in these small stretches before she's gone—
we help each other through
rough terrain, companions again.

Either way won't last long.
We'll come always to closeness,
to the unbearable tearing of it.

After Days of Rain

Three nights in a row, a full moon
blasts in our windows,
taking sleep. Before it wanes,
we wake one morning
to a thin wafer of blessing
hung in washed blue.

Winter crawls to its end.
When the cold descends again
briefly, the willows, their catkins
already turned from gray
to expectant yellow, wait.
The hawk resumes her place
at the highest point on the alder.

ANNE

when Billy Collins said, you can't really
write about the Holocaust

In the nights of insomnia I read
Anne Frank's biography.
Wading through this crush
of authenticated facts, her portrait
since birth, nothing changes
from the diary itself. A bright,
talkative, hard-to-handle, audacious,
obnoxious teenager, bordering on genius,
is going to die—faceless—at the end.

Her father—because he couldn't bear to part
with her—didn't send her to England
when he had the chance. Three weeks later,
the Nazi trap was sprung in Holland.
He sees her the last time in a selection line.

She has her clothes then. Later, head shaved,
pubic hair shaved, her beautiful innocence revealed—
which wanted all in good time, a bed
lit with afternoon sun, one sweet
article of clothing shed after the next,
a boy just that naive
and head over heels in love.

My sleepless brain refuses the lists
of details—where Anne's mother's brothers are in the U.S.,
that second cousin in Switzerland,
the year the Nazis made the Jews stay home after 8 p.m.,
the year they weren't allowed into movie theaters,

the year they couldn't ride bikes, couldn't own bikes,
the year 569,355 yellow stars were stitched, issued and worn—
a small galaxy—
the step-by-step squeeze
which wasn't, no, still wasn't death.

Smart and aware, Otto chose the wrong country.
That's all, something he couldn't have known—
but had the rest of his life to grieve.

For me, sleep, so long evasive,
suddenly appears: *take me now or forget it,*
and I switch out the light—

prized, courted sleep,
the sleep I slept at Anne's age—
the way my daughter sleeps now—
heavy, unshakable,
mornings forever.

∾

Daylight. I wake in a sweat;
each noise brings a new wave
of hot and cold.
Get up. Get up.

But the heavy limbs won't go into my clothes,
I can't get breakfast, everything's burning,

and my daughter,
my entering-teenage-daughter—
I don't put my arms around her

but gaze at her from the line
I'm forbidden to cross—to that place

I can't save her from,
even if I rush the line, and the bullet
doesn't take me from behind.

II: Tremolo

rapid reiteration of a musical tone or of alternating tones to produce a tremulous effect

And her call,
alto, cello, tremolo,
makes the life I've made melt away.
    —Ellen Bryant Voigt

TREMOLO

Beethoven's Triple Concerto in C, Opus 56,
for Violin, Cello and Piano

1.
I put the brights on, but they show
only what's there—the sanded, frost-hard road.
We ease down the hill to our evening at the symphony.

"You know that word," my daughter asks, "*tremolo*"?
"More or less," I say.
"It trembles," she says. "More than tremble."

2.
There comes a moment in the concerto's *largo*—
and all along it's been the violin telling the piano
and the piano telling it back,
the violin getting sweeter and sweeter as it answers
what the piano has proposed—
when the cello, reaching over the piano,
trying to get time with the violin,
doesn't anymore,
the cellist simply bending
over the huge awkward box he's been given,
more than he can handle,
defying it by taking it into his arms.

3.
Just the days of the week: Thursday, Saturday,
Monday, ordinary days passing out of winter,
but she and I have crossed again
into strange country.

I've watched her bundle together
my careful years of giving
and holding, listening, and no matter what,
staying on clear ground with her,
two hikers lifting our arms to air and sun—
she's knotted that together
and laid it in the lap of a boy.

"We couldn't ask for a nicer, more intelligent boy,"
my husband says, a boy who has no sense of what
he's receiving except his matching hunger.

4.
Do I think I am past this? Immune?
Having spent my bright coins of first kisses
on the boy whose last name was Swan—mine was Feathers—
in the backseat of his friend's car—

while in the front seat, the friend seduced his girl.
On our first date, we were shocked into laughing,
but not deterred—teaching each other to kiss—

Upstairs in bed now, I shield myself with my husband,
while on our couch from the forties, bearing its
many bodies, our daughter and her boy
learn with abandon the mouth's other language.

5.
As we walked her, newborn, we sealed kisses
carefully on her soft spot,
radiating its brain heat just below our chins.

Months later, she set her open, ready mouth
on ours: it was only form
we had taught her.

6.
"I'm playing those in my clarinet piece—*tremolos*,"
she says as we drive next day to the music contest.

I see the first *o* is pronounced *uh*,
almost a grunt, but needed
to move the word forward.

She's worked a year for her turn
before the judge, that moment
when the body goes hollow and clean,
waiting, trembling, to be filled with the first note
which can't falter, but must seem
as if it's always been there—
her clarinet merely pointing the way.

In James Baldwin's story, *tremolo* is stage light
quivering in the drinks on the piano
as two estranged brothers move toward each other.

Tremolo's a flame, struck tall by a sudden draft
from the night. Or the quaking aspen of my girlhood—
leaves giving way without letting go—

one note, or two alternating notes, repeated—
not as a trill which claims its own space
outside the melody's rhythm,

making us stop to admire it—
but notes repeated *in time*
and therefore tremulous:

dependent on our carrying through
to the end—a pure *oh* we hold
as long as we can.

Deposition

It's not a story-telling process,
my attorney reminds me.

Today
I'm in a dress and stockings,
careful make-up,
even lipstick.
I am asked if it's too stuffy.
Would I like something to drink?
No one is allowed to smoke.

If this were Poland
midway last century,
I would be starving,
freezing,
sleepless,
naked.

If this were Bosnia last year,
I would be brought in, raped
under blinding light,
and the questioning
would go on even
during the rape.

Nevertheless, he begins.
Did you say?
Would you assert to be true?
Did you believe?
Would you think?
Can you tell when?
tell who?
tell how?

In the tiny electric shocks
of his relentless questions
which I may not, under law,
refuse to answer, I've lost
where he might be going,
I don't know how many times
I've contradicted myself,
or where my story disappeared
in the myriad tiny fragments
of *yes*
no
I can't remember
That's not what I meant.

And the glowing cigarette
drawn by sucked-in breath
to its hottest point
seems to glide from his mouth
to my bare arm.

Paper after paper
the court has subpoenaed from me,
opened like my dress, my calendar
revealing the secret comfort
of my body to everyone.

There is lunch.
The blur of questioning
after lunch.
There is my doubt.
His legal partner
begins *her* questions.
The knowledge rises in me
I have lost my side

of what happened forever.
And the lies I've stumbled into—
which the written record's
cunning sequence
will later reveal.

Persistent April sun
clambers to get past
the windows.
There is the break
my attorney arranges for me,
the date for my next deposition.
The final click of heels
as we exit the room.

You, Teacher

Last day. First student in your office.
"I'm in a hurry," she says.
Her friend's husband has hanged himself,
and she's got to get home,
across the mountains to Richland.
"He was only seventeen."
Her tears spill over. The friend's baby,
coming in two weeks,
will have no father.

She wants her grade.
You give it, have to—her D+.
"Well, I passed," she says,
"I passed."

You use her story a few times,
put horror on your colleagues' faces—
your cheap thrill to combat the deadness
which settles after students' last frantic efforts
to make even poor work count.

Student after student files in,
the ones who tried, still amazed
that mere words can move them,
the others—angry, sad, incredulous—
their efforts reduced to one letter.
A young man, near failing,
ends your day: "Well, that's fair."

You can't bring back the afternoon
the class sat together, new leaves
emerging out of sun and shadow.
Their talk of what they'd read

came easy—even humor—
and the meaning of a story stepped
from the thicket, visible, clear.

The hour over,
everyone scattered to their commitments,
you with nothing to show for it now
except your office
stacked with stale paper.

"Goodbye," you say, "good luck,"
and carry home your empty briefcase,
no proof you've even been.

Teacher, tell now what you patch together:
their bodies so easily set their wills aside—
a baby taking hold—he's too young,
his wife's too young and clutches at him
in her fear—

drunk, he's drunk enough he tries to hang himself,
at the last minute wants to wrench away,
stumbles or pulls too tight.

Entrusted, teacher, with what your student
has given, draw that young man's body
into your arms, cradle it,
lay it tenderly down.

Take your arms away then.
Let him go, let him be.

GERÜCHE

smells

When I begin with the linden trees lining our walk,
Mechthild says their incense
is the memory of her grandparents' house
welcoming her—first grandchild.
Five godmothers each gave her a name.
Five names like gifts: she was rich as Sleeping Beauty.

We dream in the lindens.

When I point out smell as lightning rod
to memory, she nods.
The other smell I remember,
she says, *is the one of the bodies
burning after the bombing of Dresden.
That smell hung over the city for months.*

I can't say anything then.

She goes on: *Vor allem war ich allein.*
She's told me before. She was twenty-three
when the bombs took her parents. Even so,
she felt herself a girl, bereft. *Beraubt.*
Since I was young, I haven't had a mother—

She keeps going, a woman who rarely speaks:
*I know I lost my first baby
because Mother wasn't there
to tell me something was wrong
soon enough to get a doctor.*

I remember one of Mechthild's daughters
has told me that she and Mechthild

haven't held each other enough.
Her own daughter has chided her for keeping distant.

The sulphur smell from my mother's body
as I readied her for cremation—regret
that in her last weeks, we didn't
make up the dearth of our holding.

Toward the end, I say to Mechthild,
I couldn't slide my arms
under her brittle vertebrae, her pain
acute, terrible.

For the first time since I've known her,
Mechthild reaches up to me,
her hands cradling my face a moment long.

Holding is the only way not to speak.
Her baby might have died anyway,
but Mechthild's mother could have put her arms
around her shoulders, let the sobs
course through them both,
until they quieted.

Nootka

Peninsula wild rose

I'm learning to balance
on the roadside bank,
teetering at the edge
where the bramble sprawls,

and the full force
of the roses' scent
can reach me.

After I'm quiet enough,
the swallows—gray, blue, gold—
resume their swoop and dive
for insects.

One petal near me loosens
to fall; in the thick of bloom,
one bud unfolds.

I'm suspended
as neither bird nor flower
seem to be.

BEECH

Where there are beech trees, the land is always beautiful.
    —a phrase from Richard Jeffries, given me by my
        friend Bob Pyle, a foremost butterfly expert

Rain had soaked you, Bob,
as you scrambled down a hillside
in Switzerland, beeches opening their leaves
like an overture to Beethoven.

Hungry, not because you were,
but because you were almost out of money—
all that lay between you and want.

You couldn't work up courage to visit
the great Nabakov and talk butterflies.
What would you have to say?
"I'll come back," you promised yourself.
Before you could, he was dead.

How many times I've gone that same distance
in a foreign country, found what I've hungered for,
but couldn't ready myself
to brave the stares and break silence
with rasped, clotted speech—
a near miss of how words
in another language should sound.

Regret. Unable to discharge debt,
your life became
what you didn't have a chance to tell him.

Half an hour to visit the viewpoint at *Königstuhl,*
and my companions, far ahead, anxious to see
what the guidebook promised.
I dawdled as always,
hoping something would speak.

Nothing could match our Northwest firs,
I scoffed—but disdain can open a space.

Around me the smooth gray of the giant beech trunks,
their unreachable canopy, filtering light,
a kind of silence: holding fast
the chalk cliffs above the Baltic.

I was standing where Friedrich stood
when he painted sea and jagged rock, framed
by these sheltering beeches—a Romantic painting,
the trees *guardians*, keeping
his three wanderers from the edge.

Buchenwald—beech forest. The one
near Weimar no different in its hundred-foot trees
rising in full, trembling leaf.

Buchen, hollow and breathy,
wind in the highest branches,
point of no return. But *Wald* brings me back,
and I lean into the trees, trunk to trunk.

A word can be tied by torment
to so many things opposite of tree and leaf,

of bare branch and breaking forth
from green-gold, red-brown bud—
that to say it
is to break a certain kind of faith
with those who heard it as death.

Which break, then, must be rescued
from silencing.

Say *Buchenwald*, beech forest,
bearing its necessary other burden,
where human blood's been soaked indelibly,
denied spirits still calling.

Say *Buchenwald*. Without its sound,
we might forget this forest.
Trees don't need to speak. We do.

CROSSING PUGET SOUND

My dad is gradually turning to stone.
Stroke has stopped his hands like cooling lava.
Nothing moves voluntarily.

We poke his arm into sleeve, foot into underwear.
When I rub his arms, his head—
I feel granite emerging.

All week my other language hangs
the word at the back of my throat: *versteinern.*
Stein—stone—buried within.

I look to see if I've got
the right German word.
Then I see the English: *petrify.*

Pressed against the railing on the lower car deck
this late summer night,
I'm watching the diagonal line of white water

surge away where the ferry cuts through.
Once raised, the water won't stop
until it slaps against some calm inland beach

and makes a difference there.
I crossed the Sound first with him,
long ago, and now I've crossed

so many times without him,
water rising at night
is my own uncertain journey.

Every day my brother gets him up,
dresses, shaves, feeds him,
bandages skin no longer able to hold a body.

We imagine life as upright,
eyes open, letting the world
our brain delivered in sleep

disintegrate with breakfast talk:
there I was hitchhiking on a country road
with Randy and a squalling baby.

When my brother holds the phone
to Dad's ear and I shout to his deafness,
"Goodnight, Dad," he often answers,

"Goodnight, Alice." But now
I've come to visit, he calls me *Violet*,
a name I don't know.

We tuck him in. He seems so much
like a child settling down,
I plant a row of kisses on his forehead.

When I look up,
his mouth is poised and ready.
He kisses me three times.

Saturday mornings, he and my mother
kissed so loudly we kids in our single beds
could hear them down the hall.

He relished it.
After I was five, I don't think he kissed me
until I was married, safe.

"Can you remember Rock Creek?"
my brother shouts at him.
"Nope."

"Can you remember Canby?"
"Nope."
Only the bright interrogation lights are missing.

Hour after hour he stares into silence,
as he did whole evenings
of my girlhood. I wasn't allowed

to interrupt. Under the lamp,
he read Indian history he revered,
then raised his head to wait

for words, his next day's lecture.
I wanted to be close to him
in that brightness, his eyes on me.

∿

Grief refreshes itself
in the days we're just coasting,
then takes us again.

If I stare too long, lean out
too far, I remember
I'm scared of black water—

it took me years
to get over the fear I had as a kid
when the ferry approached its oiled pilings.

No matter how well the boat imitated
firm ground, I could see it drifted
at the water's pleasure.

Shivering out here tonight, the ferry
groaning under the steady throb
of its engines, I'm afraid again.

I might fall in, or jump, toss
my car keys overboard, something
irretrievable, final, before we get across.

III: Grace Note

ornamental notes not included in the sum of notes in the bar; Chopin wrote long chains of grace notes, to be performed lightly and freely while maintaining a steady tempo

I try to listen in that way, the grace notes
on the underside of sound.
—Lorna Crozier

PRECARIOUS

John Singer Sargent

Jews as celebration.

You made one Wertheimer daughter
a Turkish musician, another, a gypsy
holding her broomstick. Several, sheathed
in red, lips bright, eyes defying any of us
to get a life.

You weren't just taunting the anti-Semitism
your rich British clients wanted to hide
when you brought these paintings
audaciously close to royal portraiture.
You let the family invite you over for supper,
sat with them, became friends.

Mrs. G's slipping shoulder strap
forced you to leave Paris. After you'd ingratiated
yourself with her. She, just as attracted.
Ground you'd gained for a decade lost over the scandal.

But your clients didn't trust the camera—so lately
in fashion. They depended on you for eternity.
Who could resist *not* giving them what they hungered for?

Still, you didn't rub their faces in the life-sized male nudes
crowding this gallery: nude after nude after nude.
Giving myself twenty minutes to come to grips
with that many genitals
that baldly hung,
I surrender to the sweet exuberance of the bodies,
tenderly vulnerable.

And how you *use* them, sprawled in every compromising pose
for your voyeurism, your lust.
"Was he a lover of women?" your critics keep asking
(archly) as late as 1957.

You saved the glittering African girl from Crete
to hang on your own walls.
You turned the body of the black man, Thomas McKellar,
into a Greek god for the Boston library murals.
I doubt if you were just thumbing your nose at secret racism.
You'd fallen in love with a shape.
As one might fall in love with rolling hills.

In the portrait of him as him, he opens his legs in trust,
his eyes hold steady
while his penis lolls to one side,
as a penis does after pleasure.

My eyes are caught in the middle of his huge body,
mortified that being human
means a mind to reason us
out of brutal desire—yet it can't.

So that nothing I see today is head on
but bears its undeniable
double blade.

You weren't Van Gogh, living hand to mouth,
painting exactly how you saw things,
to heck with scorn.
You wanted to be great *and* successful.

Your neighbor Oscar Wilde
had paid the price. And after you were gone,

Ruby—youngest Wertheimer, the child
whose deep eyes follow us here—
was singing opera in Italy
when the Nazis detained her, killed her.

Before I leave these rooms,
I study the 1910 photo of you painting outside,
Swiss Alps behind you. Mustached, gone to fat,
vest, coat and hat—you've got yourself
covered, the artist as we imagine him.

And then—I can't help myself—I go back through
the paintings again—the verve of them, the daring.

The Planet Closest To Us

Mourning begins in a kind of thick non-seeing,
only later clarified, gradually lightening,
until we recognize what our lives must carry.

As we drove the three hours to Seattle,
our van was always moving toward light,
but maybe dawn never is a *moment.*

On a good day I gradually come to,
thought by thought climbing
into the waking world,
not bolting upright over a missed deadline
or scenes of someone's death: my mother's.

Toward the light—faith that it will come
lets us look forward, our dead also
no more than thought.

All the time keeping up my share of talk
with my colleagues, while the van
veered from curve to curve, what I watched
was the morning star, blazing
even in a sky blurred by rain.

We've chosen the planet closest to us,
third brightest after sun and moon,
hanging seductively in sunset's orange,
or now, burning into the black cold of January—

Even in its unacceptable heat and atmosphere,
we've named our small companion
for the attachment we long most for:
love, a kind of opening.

In the hard nights I can list so clearly
the places she went wrong with me,
no gentleness there, as the years fade
toward acceptance.

We were never *with* each other, companions,
and now she is so often with me,
her arms stilled by stroke,
her voice smothered. I had to lean close
and nothing for it,
because she was leaving.

WINGS,

their primary feathers spread like fingers,
stage the balancing act of seven turkey vultures
fanned over a field. I can't look up
to follow their passing, deep into the drive

along Dungeness fields I've known for years—
Weyerhauser seed trees, wheat in its circular rows
matching the way a cultivator moves, the test in me
to rise with each plant's transformation, to climb

out of winter and the last edges of a deep-seated virus.
To take strength. I've never seen Old World swans fly,
only the heavy curve of their bodies on European ponds,

bearing their proud, masked heads. Nothing hidden,
these vultures' dark flame burns clear, poised
at a sign to drop down, begin with another's end.

SWEET LIPS, CLEAR EYES
Holde Lippen, klares Auge

> *Berlin, 2007: Britta Süberkrüb sings a Schumann*
> *Lieder Cycle: The Love and Life of Women*

She descends the shivering low notes—
Ich kann's nicht fassen—I can't grasp his love.

Summer rain beats on this crumbling villa
in West Berlin, the neighborhood
I walked as a student forty years ago.

Surrounded by a language only half intelligible,
struggling to make it seamless,
I learned to listen.

Even now, sound flashes ahead, striking, jubilant
across her mezzo soprano,
before the meaning floods me.

Laß der feuchten Perlen
Ungewohnte Zier
Freudig hell erzittern
In dem Auge mir.

German's tight syntax wraps its package
in the smallest number of words.
I learned to wear its ravel,

no longer needing to restring
English's many, straightforward strands.

A woman's tears of joy tremble in her eyes,
luminous as pearls. Let them be,
she tells her lover,
my unaccustomed adornment.

Not the ideas but how she sings them.

Her beauty's lit from within. She sets love
before us in its spangled box and ribbons,
stilling her fingers to make anticipation last.

We lean toward her as she lifts the lid,
her voice urged to its final, headlong rise.

FOR MORRIS GRAVES
FROM A NOVITIATE

I have stopped trying to say anything
about anything—there is no statement
or message other than the presence
of the flowers and light—that is enough.
—Morris Graves, 1980

1.
Your paintings remind us
of what's not given—
but flowers as I know them
hold nothing back.

When I wander the high ridge
in summer, meadows
crammed with lupine and painted cup
race toward their blooming.

Buds unfold, insects wing in,
air moves light. Dazzle:
sense of a step beyond—
sheer extravagance just for the heck of it.

Even in my garden, flowers
are framed by their *background*—
iris blades, bleeding heart's
lace, the hosta's platters.

You've pressed your kindled blossoms
against stained walls,
or stuck them in dirty corners,
stripped of leaves.

Pigment stands in for light.
Blooming makes all the hope there is.

2.

> *I don't walk; I stagger.*
> *Spring knocks me out.*
> . . . .
> *You flowers*
> *have pity on a white-haired man.*
> —Tu Fu, 8th Century

I can't be part of your Eastern connection.
Sorry. I've tried. I don't go without,
having tasted austerity's offerings
when I was a child and had no choice.

I just want, and give in to wanting,
squander what I've got, and live with
disappointments piling up, some days cloud-deep
until night's insomnia and wrestling.

3.

> *But take that vase*
> *of lilacs: who goes*
> *near it is erased.*
> —Kay Ryan, "That Vase of Lilacs," 1996

I come back to this room of paintings
because you have it right—
the way flowers glow.

Especially indoors they refuse to let
a person be. Best, your winter bouquet
of hellebore and rosehaws,

the bare stems hung with orange-red suns
to keep lit all winter. I like too
the tiny halo of strawberry blossoms

in this still life of poverty: leeks,
Morton's salt, a few wizened apples,
calendar's solstice outlined in red.

I can't get loose.
Stopped near vases of lilacs or dahlias,
I'll try to express them as they do light.

They'll be themselves, on fire
with their urgency. Brush stroke
by brush stroke, you return their heat.

ELEPHANTS

A sahib has got to act like a sahib;
he has got to appear resolute; to know
his own mind and do definite things. . . .
But I did not want to shoot the elephant.
　　　　—George Orwell, "Shooting an Elephant"

I like the twenty elephants best.
My three-year old, talking to me all week
about elephants, has fallen asleep in my arms.
She's missing how they circle
the tent's largest ring, kneel, then rise,
their forelegs lifted to the next one's back.

I like elephants for their thick gray skin
hanging in comfortable folds.
Their size, which makes up for the fact
they're not as flashy as the tigers.
Their intelligence rivaling the gorilla's.
Holding memory of *savannah*,
their brown eyes might wonder
at the hoopla here.

I see the chains holding them too.
But the glitter on the costumes
of the high trapeze flyers fixes the light
in my eyes. This Asian family's pride is fierce.
They zoom through air, and trained past grief,
land upright, their arms open to applause.

Last night on TV, young father, mother,
two small children. Evicted. Living
in their car. They sleep at the airport
where their son can watch
the planes take off and land.

My small one stirs in her sleep,
full of cotton candy, and still believing
the wonder. I want her to learn gradually
that the circus is less than magic,
more than pain.

She's not fooled. Last night at dinner,
she listened as we mourned a cousin's
early dying. Her eyes drew in mother, father,
grandparents. "I'll be ok," she said.
"They're not my people." Aware
that she guarded herself.

When the show's over, she wakes.
Even though it's raining outside, she wants
to watch the elephants. She tells me how
they eat, roll in the mud, lift dirt
and shower it over themselves.

Before her first year was out,
she was helping herself to as many words
as she could. She'd talk to keep track
of what was missing too.
"Use your words," we say now
when she cries. "Tell us."

I Mean *Beach, Fir, Yellow*

1.
A ridge isn't what you'd think,
level on top while all the struggle
falls to either side. It's a steady rise
and fall and rise through fir and pine,
then meadows, then up into the scree,
the last steep scramble for the view.

Climbing the ridge to Maiden Peak,
we're like the medieval saints, separated
by halos, ours of buzzing deer flies.
Record snowfall has bent the turrets of subalpine fir
to *krummholz*. Out of their lockstep order,
they reel topsy-turvy down the slopes.

It's avalanche lily time.
We already know when we cross
from the ridge's south-side, warmth releasing
the heady scent of lodgepole needles,
lilies will have seized their northern meadows.

Six-sided stars, each center stained yellow—
under full sun, like comets, they streak
up the hill; in hemlock's deep shadow,
spread out like constellations; or burn
their little wells of growing space
into the melting snow. As deeply
as I want to look, they'll reveal.

2.
Which doesn't mean I can see them
past suppertime.
These words I've carefully set down
to be their witness
have found another story—
boots marching across a continent,
trampling a whole people
who wore their stars like muffled light.

What I recall with startling accuracy
is whether a hike brought our family closer
or undid us.

Once when heavy snow blocked
our climb to a crater's rim, we got out food
and picnicked on a fallen fir, told
old stories, let the sun spread heat
around us—husband, wife, daughter,
together and loving it.

Those survivors beating back Fascism
faced years and years of sleepless nights.
What happened then and then and *then*—
they sit up in bed, fending off blows.

3.
Last month the coast—azure sky,
ocean in its rhythms, seastacks fading to haze,

wind. We teetered on cobbles in the smell
of seaweed baked at low tide.

All I have now is my story.

I pile up words, saying, *beach, fir,*
lily, yellow. I mean the dazzle of light
that takes me, tired from camping
and too-tight boots, and turns me into
breaking surf, into sea-star.

But even sand the ocean has beaten
into receiving water without resistance,
still resists. This beach won't let me write it down.
Those survivors: not everyone could be killed.

Like photos of our trip, stilled, pristine—
words bring back the ache
without the things themselves.

Nevertheless, the refugees from genocide
huddle about their saved words,
untying the knotted bundles:

bread, sun slanting through the new linden leaves,
a daughter's crown of black curls
when she appears against the treeline
walking home from school.

IV: Cantabile

singable, a term often used by Beethoven to qualify
slow or moderate movements

Ay! Like the bow of a viola
the cry vibrates
long strings of wind.
    —Federico Garcia Lorca, "Poem of the Deep Song"
    (trans. Ralph Angel)

WAKING, WALKING, SINGING IN THE NEXT DIMENSION
—Morris Graves

> *On to the fields of praise.*
> —Dylan Thomas, "Fern Hill"

1.
It doesn't matter, Morris Graves,
that your three circles of white
are unmistakeable: one, the soul as it's
handed to the body, intact, but startled,
an owl staring into sudden light.
Women giving birth have watched
their child at the moment of fusion.

White is darkest in your circle of bird walking—
like a third grader's penmanship practice
as she teaches her hand to give itself
to the cursive flow of round.

In a final flourish at the end of her page,
she leaves the teacher's direction
to see how her ovals might lift off and fly—
your paint in the third circle
folds up to become a kind of fabric,
the edge of a sheer curtain in light breeze.

Unlikely rainbows burst through to haunt the white.

Your bird, no longer definite,
raises its head and sings. Whatever we think,
we've stepped into the next dimension.

2.
Color—and you've made white a color—
is the painting's reason.
Your rubbed-out background of gray and brown
shimmers, illuminates. Pink, peach, rose.
These are the unlikely tones you offer us
for treading the spirit's unstable ground.

You know color as birds know flight,
out of necessity,
when something inside signals.

3.
Each of our recent days, snow revealing them,
eight or nine thrushes storm the downed hemlock
where I scatter seed. Flurry of their bickering,
then rush to refuge in the young madrones,
bodies only for moments

like that stillness, summers at Hurricane Ridge,
when gray jays land on my outstretched palm
for a gift of raisins.

Today I wait by the kitchen window,
watching the flicker stab beak-deep into
soft suet. A sound, a change: it stops,
then barrels into the woods,
rust of its tail's underside flashing.

Thrush feathers too—folded grey on orange,
grey on orange—blur to motion,
leaving me with my hunger.

Once the thrushes retreat
to the cedars, their high clear solos
break into the cold, each bird, one note,
drawn out until it fades, as it has to.
In the silence—what we depend on—
the treble sound again, again.

VISITING THE ELGIN MARBLES, 2007

for my daughter

Their heads are gone.
Most of their arms too.
Demeter and Persephone

touch knee to knee,
as we often sit.
Their solid trunks lean

forward, this murmured
conversation meant
only to draw them closer.

The fabric of their robes
drapes so lightly
its folds nearly sway.

Easy to fill in what's missing:
Persephone's returned
to broad summer light.

An evening could last forever—
except for the haze
rising in the distance.

This season will end,
but not like the first time.
Who could take in the cut

of Hades' flashing wheels?
A field of flowers
where a girl had been.

In the Fields

flaming yellow lit acre after acre, crowding the squares of still-green wheat,
threaded with wild poppies. Late spring, my family bicycled
crisscrossing farm lanes

around Göttingen—the rolling hill country of central Germany—
then aimed toward the medieval guard towers
and crumbling *Burg* beyond.

When I asked what the yellow was, *Raps*, our friends said. I looked up
the English: *rape.* How could rape be this simple mustard
grown for cooking oil?

Another friend's story startles me now, a specter in the rainy night.
We hurtle toward Portland, and she tells me
she was raped at thirteen,

staying overnight with a pal, hide and seek in the dark alley,
neighbor boy stepping from the square of yellow light
which marked a doorway:

C'mon, I wanna show you something. "That's when I lost my sense
of boundaries," she goes on. "When I quit getting straight A's
and eventually just quit."

As soon as you cross between languages, exchanging one word
for another, safety dissolves. No matter how
you've buried your grief

in the sounds you love, the world sits on the back fence,
wordless and whole, licking its coat in the sunshine,
daring you.

Gift in German, after all, means poison, what might be offered
under cover of dark. Drawn by a magnet in the giddy nights
of early adolescence,

my friend crossed the dim lawn since no one was there
to wrap a warning arm around her shoulder,
He's not thinking about you.

English and German were almost one language when Latin
brought them *raps.* Centuries later, the Normans
infused their French—*rapere*, to seize.

Rape flickered its double tongue. Split away, German's *Vergewaltigung.*
It takes enough breath, makes enough noise.
Buried inside, *Gewalt*, violence.

Who can keep the well-cared-for fields intact? Say rape and you
hear the scream. *Have you seen my purse?* a woman shouts
as she streams past me

in a café. Her wrenched face has nothing to do
with a red handbag. She spills from the top of her tight,
leopard-print dress,

in some way offering herself to the security officer, trying vainly
to help. Chained to a scene from her girlhood, her body
can't find its bearings.

Generations of slave women in master's bed. Korean "comfort" girls,
sold by their parents—forty men claimed their turns
the first day alone.

In Darfur, village daughters are burned to cover their spoilage.
Five soldiers in Baghdad took the girl over and over,
then killed her entire family.

Seed is drilled into the damp earth. Without volition, ground
blazes its yield across the horizon. *How dazzling,*
my family said of the fields,

how beautiful. The beauty of her singing led Tereus to steal his wife's
sister, Philomela, and rape her. He cut out Procne's tongue
so she couldn't tell the story.

The gods turned all three into birds. Nightingale worries a passionate
spring evening. In the fields of vibrant color what is broken
remains mute.

ARMOR

another Nazi sweep begins

A woman takes up her needle,
the colors building themselves
into gardens of refuge
where her hands have work to do
and she can wander, forget.

Gathered around this woman's husband,
the men say to themselves,
she's in the next room, sewing.
They don't think of someone sewing
as someone.

She doesn't want to be listening either,
hasn't wanted a morning
like this to arrive, to have to tell
her husband she's going out just
shortly, a brief errand before lunch,
a friend is ill, dressing so carefully,
lips precise, the fur coat—
thank goodness for winter—like armor.

To have to tell her driver she'll
go in and choose the bouquet herself:
Don't wait. But come back—
right here—in twenty minutes.
If he's questioned, the driver can say
what he knows: *she went into the florist's.*

She wants to call on the young doctor
at the moment between his receptionist
leaving and his stepping out.
Herr Doktor, saying it softly but clearly

as she stands beneath him on the steps,
and he turns, smiles to see her,
wants to turn back, let her in.

Not to be seen even laying
a gloved hand on his arm,
yet to hold him with her eyes:
Herr Doktor, tomorrow I won't see you.
Sorry, I won't see you.

Of course you will if you wish.
Or today. There are still appointments.

"*I won't see you tomorrow,*" she has to repeat
firmly but not more loudly.

The question now in his eyes,
he nods politely, tips his hat,
walks home to his wife and new baby.

His patient returns to her husband.
After he has closed himself
into his office, she takes up her sewing,
making each flower precise in the wild
array, each leaf alive until a long strand
might seem like Eden.

You've gotten on the wrong path
if you think there was something between her
and the young doctor. There was.
That he was not her lover. That she came

to be treated for nerves, and a man
didn't close down at her tumbled words,
thinking, *what a waste.*

∾

The doctor rocks his baby
while his wife serves the soup.
Then his free hand closes over his wife's in mid-air.
"Now," he says. "Don't talk.
One suitcase. The baby in
her bunting so she won't be noticed.
A train leaves for Prague in an hour."

∾

Prague still open, the Jewish doctor
receives his life.

Drawing curtains against the evening,
the woman moves to her chair.
She's left a kind of garden,
stepped into a street full of risky strangers.
Now her hands rest again on the flowers,
but she doesn't turn on the lamp.

When the war ends, part of the enemy herself,
she'll be a refugee in her own country,
each day requiring a kind of iron will she's never
had—thin soup, cold rooms.
Nothing a thread could carry.

Her husband gets ready to go out,
sliding his gun from its felt-lined drawer
into the inner satin pocket of his coat.
"Don't wait up," he says.

His Own

Fred plays Haydn's Concerto #2 in D Major
for Cello and Orchestra

> *He has to fill it, this instrument,*
> *with the breath of life, his own.*
> —James Baldwin, "Sonny's Blues"

Swimming. The word Baldwin doesn't say
for all of "Sonny's Blues." He makes
the reader say it, the difference
between deep water and drowning.
Sonny, playing for his life.

You said to me, "Haydn's like a deep ocean—
my tiny boat tossed about."

I guess that means your incessant racing
up and down the fingerboard, your bow
going at it more like a mattock
in the hands of a Van Gogh peasant
determined to make spring happen.

"A few good harbors," you promised me.

They are sweetness I can hardly stand
and dissonance way beyond Haydn's time—
what I came for, of course, out-of-body travel:

like making love this morning with my husband,
ecstatic waves sounding again and again
on my body's shore until I left our bed
for the open sea.

∾

While the orchestra was getting us started,
before you began to play,
I could see you lean into your solo,
remembering the part of reality
you had to make stick.
Music doesn't just hang in air.

I don't want you to stop playing.
I don't want to flee with Sonny's dad,
escaping down an unlighted street
after a car of drunken whites runs over his brother.

All this time later, it's not as if
black people were our neighbors
so we could be borrowing back and forth,
saying good morning, until one day
we'd need each other and be there.

When you and I read Baldwin essays,
the pain of three centuries
stepped into the dim Sunday parlor
where all of us spent our childhoods,
learning what lay under the talk
adults flashed by us.

Over the years I've made my pilgrimage
through the black writers, hoping to learn
their lives as well as I need to.

Sometimes they've sat with me,
speaking of ways to let slavery's grief,
like water, carry light.

We still look for a crossing.

When you stopped playing,
silence welcomed into itself the fading overtones,
both of us listening.

FOOLING AROUND

at the high school state music contest

In the aging hotel pool, I'm doing laps.
Around the smaller pool, lit from the bottom,
a director has arranged her dozen adolescents,
water-light shining up into their faces.

Hardly grown herself,
you guys, she calls her students,
gauze blouse over a tight camisole.
Her feet bare to the wet tile,
as if water might be necessary
to making music.

Using the only space open this night
before the contest, she goes as far
as she can. Even while they're singing,
her charges sign to each other, dance,
lift chairs, high-kick, roam.
When she has them clap the rhythm
to make it part of themselves,
one beats his head on the wall in perfect time.

And if she cuts them off to say *No!*
or *Fortissimo!* or *it swings there*,
they take up—as if they've never stopped—
their stream of talk focused on each other.

I quit swimming and openly gape,
but she directs with her whole body.
I can't tell when she gives the downbeat,

only when the *alleluias* fall in ovals
out of which the harmony rises—

not a seed's green opening
slowly transfigured, but fully formed,

the angel filling Mary's room with election,
where the young self trembles in love.

The soprano of this group floats way up there,
surprising herself each time.
She stays after their teacher dismisses them,
fooling around—
because when she opens her mouth
tones drift to the water like leaves.

She can't imagine what she might become,
growing up in a desert small-town,
an outpost on the latest volcanic effusion
spreading over Eastern Washington.

Maybe what surrounded the exquisite coloratura
in my country college
couldn't grant a way forward either.

She was the girl I wanted to be, her gift
riding my shoulder with its heavy hand.
When she sang, our choir director's taunts
softened, and we reached through vast unknowing.

A few years later, I saw her again—
what smoking and drink had done,
and the wrong man—her voice gone to gravel.

Maybe people don't want to be chosen.

The simple girl of Nazareth
visited by an improbable angel
had already said yes to someone else.
She didn't hesitate.

Or Maria Callas.
What was there early on to sustain her
except hunger?

She would have starved
if she hadn't said *yes*.

Saying yes.
Using her voice to the last.
When it was taken, long before
her life was over,
living with that too.
Even that.

V: Turn

four notes encircling the main note

The chain of transformations questions more and more the character of each variation. It is a great process of dissolving into which we are drawn. . . .
—Hans Mersmann on the last movement of Beethoven's Opus 111

At that specific point [of music], emotion has staggered into inarticulacy beyond the boundaries of language. . .
—Brian Friel

THROUGH FIELD GLASSES

Beach camping: it's real and not.
Seals like abandoned logs on the far rocks,
but if I squint through the glasses, they tip heads

and tails up, come alive. My daughter works
sea glass among the shingles. My husband's
finding the memorial to the Norwegian

shipwreck, a tragedy from 1905. Stalled
under this benevolent July sun, the three of us
laze in a contentment we pretend could last.

Two sea otters. One rides the surface,
stretched on its back, cradling its front paws,
head dry enough for the fur to ray out in an afro.

The other, probably her pup, never leaving
her side, weaves into water and out again,
a shuttle, head slicked tight as a seal's.

"I can't hear anything out here," my husband says,
"with this surf." He means he can't hear himself think.
The flag of sanderlings waves light, then dark,

and sets down, fast-running two-leggers.
Nothing lets you come close, but it's as close
as you're going to get. Same for our threesome,

having put in its nineteen years. Bound
into some unconscious necessity, only rarely
amicable, but fierce, like the juvenile eagle

we startled from a cove early this morning.
Wings spanned, it seemed for a second to lumber,
then flashed high, the parent right on its tail.

Now, in a matter of minutes, we've fumbled
our stove, dumped over the lunch noodles.
Our daughter trips on a root, cutting her leg.

Not paying attention, I've lost my only hat.
Tears, exasperation, as if this were serious,
as if we couldn't get out of the wind

against a ragged spruce, and make a different lunch.
But the person who has loved me most
unequivocally is leaving. Has to, growing up.

All three taking it in stride, while what we've
given, almost without thought,
becomes a part of leaving, even of ourselves.

In a day or so, we'll walk out through the dark mile
of spruce and cedar, some trunks wider
than a person is tall. We won't talk into the silence,

our packs tipping us off balance as we negotiate
slicker parts of the trail. Where the shelter of trees
ends, we'll face light, at the road.

On the Radio, Mozart's Piano Trio #7 in G Major

Borodin Trio

Can something be made of these round moments
strung like beads
on the first spring sun with heat?

Afternoon traffic at a stand-still, stretching out
interminably the picking up of children.

Sun pours in the driver's window from a sky
once again that solid reassuring blue
until you're warmed all over—
piano and cello taking the high and low,
sweetness and foreboding
like a score for *Othello*,
each note filling you until you're happy.

Idling here, slumped in your seat,
you can't help stringing these beads
next to the towers' 3,000 dead
you haven't known how to mourn,
or the 1,000 buried alive in last week's earthquake.
Each smooth globe passes through your fingers
and is released. A bomb at Passover Seder.
As her mother is buried, her teenaged daughter
faces the cameras: *she was everything*.

Your hands repeat the litany:
daughters held down while their genitals
are mutilated, ancient ritual.
Sons betrayed by priests.

And still Mozart's notes pass over your tight-stretched
eardrum, sound wave after wave translated to vibration.

In the inner protected labyrinth, each membrane
knocks at the next one's door
until the brain takes up their humming,
and you gain entrance far inside—what you feel as *inside*—
to gardens of delight.

You, your body whole. This morning you've had
your hot shower. And your girl,
the one you work your way toward
on this grid of small town streets, she
is safe. You already know that.

All day you wear this scalding necklace,
take it off at the dressing table in the lengthening

spring evening, its weight in your fingers.
Through the open window, frogs' bright insistent chorus
announces the complications of hope.

You sit like Desdemona by candlelight, unable
to stop the fate she could see clearly
as it entered the room still filled
only with herself and Emilia.

Willow, willow, willow, she sings then, *sing
all a green willow,* as if pulling a robe close.
The notes of the song flood the night
no less than dread.

Hardhack in Bloom,

leggy, crowding its rosy plumes against the fence.
The palomino comes right to the gate.

Along Old Olympic highway, fireweed rises
in one magenta stand after the next.

That should be enough color to get started.

2.
When the Polish pianist, Piotr Anderszewski,
now living in Paris, played in Chicago last month,
we were supposed to think he *was* Chopin.

OK. I went along willingly, back to the scene
from *Masterpiece Theater,* glass doors opening
to Majorcan sunshine, palms, islands of languid flowers.

Chopin at the piano, Sand—and you get the feeling
he might have called her George—slouches
against the door frame, this the fiery decade of their affair,

the last of his life. I still want to *be* Sand,
in the most impossible love, ravenous
for his music, while he, disappearing, plays to me.

3.
The week my mother-in-law lies in hospital,
her tests gradually bringing the shadowy mass
of the first scan to lymphoma, I listen to Chopin.

It's all that helps, music which tramples, which seizes,
which takes me between its jaws and doesn't let go.

Huge, rolling chords of the romantics—
"Those strange, ground-breaking, left hand chords,"
the critic writes, "chromaticism . . . which pierces the heart."

While Anderszweski's right hand rills like creek water
over stones. Or gallops the limits of a fenced field.

4.
Already two decades since Keats had blazed forth
and was consumed, his plea for "quiet breathing"
unequivocal: to let himself be bound to earth.

"My heart aches," he begins his "Ode to a Nightingale,"
bold and direct. "Now more than ever it seems rich to die."
But he talks himself out of it by the end of the poem.

"Darkling I listen" and he means in the northern
summer dusk, which never seems to let go.
I tell you, when hardhack's in bloom

and trefoil's weedy yellow has splashed up the embankments
overwhelming the wild daisies,
when blackberries are on, and the Himalayas

begin their month-long cycle from pink muslin to green knots
to what's going to be juice in our mouths,
all the while mounted on the most terrific barbs—

so we loiter in the sun, picking until our fingers stain—
and in the ditches the patches of simple heal-all
blazon purple and true—

then summer most generous, most warm,
Keats on his way to Italy, knowing all the time
he was leaving warmth. Leaving Fanny.

Finding the Poem

after twenty-five years on the Olympic Peninsula,
we watch coho jump the Soleduck cascades

Solil'tak: Quilleute for sparkling water

"I'm good," you say, and go back to the car.
How differently we need things—

I could be here until dark comes down, or rain,
each fish making me content
to wait as long as I need to,
until the next catapults skyward.

It's not what we're allowed to call *will*,
but they're up for it,
slapping against the rocks
if their aim isn't in line with the surging down-current,
or landing in a shallow dish on top,
which leads nowhere.
A futile surge forward, then
they let themselves be washed back and down.

Some slip up the sides of this narrow chute
or sluice through. Some shoot dead center—
ruby bodies nothing but muscle,
heads iridescent green.

So much takes place below what's churned white,
I can't tell which fish make it
and which must accept over and over
a fall to slack water.

The boiling on a rock shelf,
full of thrashing tails, has to be the next step.
Maybe ten miles, all they have left
of the sixty they can reach up this river
to channels and springs of their birth and spawning.

Strands of silver stitching together our world,
my friend writes. We know their story,
carrying heart's blood high into the mountains,
feeding animals and trees
before sending their fry spiraling down
to saltwater again.

Somewhere I read how difficult it is,
their change to ocean. Like being smothered.

"Discouraging," you say, when I come to the car—
"everything's going in one direction
 and you're going in another."

"They don't feel that way," I say.
"Salmon are built for their stream."
"Ok." You let go quietly. I don't press my point
 as I usually do. "Stay as long as you want," you say.

We've lost three parents in a short time—
our arms raised, warding off blows.
We're tender with one another.

So I go back.

I go back to watch how, water-bound
and trying every other course first,
they launch and fly,

paddling air,
bringing to its indifferent pressure—its lassitude,
which can't receive hard rowing,
but asks for the lightness of bird-bone—
what they have to offer water:

mushing through
as far as they can go. Farther.

FRAGMENT

Neolithic figure,
Goulandris Museum, Athens

All that's left: her pelvis
with fingertips resting lightly
on either side.

She's alone in this museum,
surrounded by dozens of figures
from 3,000 years later.

Reach past our own two millennia—
that's history. Then back five more.
How free I imagine her—

goddess of hips and cool air.
Her laugh in the evening
embraces me like a shawl.

Maybe she will show me how to dance
on the Cretan sand. Shyly, I can
step out. When she slips

into the soft Aegean,
the path of her lifting arms lit
with phosphorescence, I follow.

PRAISE

I'm invited to be part of a Native weaving circle.
—for Theresa

My life has been lost many times.
The words of one woman lift from our talk
as waves rise with the wind on Lake Ozette.
We sit in the cabin's common room, each
with her cedar project, still receiving the tree's
original sustenance. One moment
the ancient, next we're here and now.

Seized from her grandfather in a government
"child scoop," this Canadian woman was raised
in white foster care where she could be "civilized."
The older weavers remember aloud how the schools
beat one language out of them, another in.

Like the woof of the mat I'm learning to make,
talk is coded pattern, required form,
as if they had not owned English long enough
to freight it with sorrow.
Our room seems a momentary refuge:
whites and Indians still disputing land.

The same Victorian beliefs forced
on their grandparents—*cover your nakedness*
and pray—surface in the initial tsks of shock
when our instructor brings out her whaler doll.
Dressed in black bear hide, his scanty cedar apron
barely covers his rafia penis.
Then the laughter erupts, *God, he's one ball short!*

While hands do what they know,
banter and teasing begin, jokes peaking higher,
then higher. Then the fall. Time makes cedar—

worked over and under without ceremony,
or any sense of *start now, end now*—a hat,
dropping into the room.

We weave, piecing together the story
this woman tells, trying to understand
why her son had to take his life.

When she was six, her mother left her.
Lost then to her grandfather. White teachers
with their mission. Despair will have
its outcome, one generation or the next.

Don't be sentimental, I warn myself.
Don't eulogize where eulogy isn't called for.
No, these women force each one to bear
what she's got and keep at it.

How nice your mat looks, they tell me.
That's just beautiful, says the elder.
I praise too, our words still symbols
of the parting gifts we place in each other's hands:
prepared seaweed, wind-dried salmon,
herring eggs, Indian tea, apples.

Notes to the Poems

Quotations about Beethoven and Chopin were taken from CD jacket notes: Deutsche Grammophon, *The Late Piano Sonatas* played by Raurizio Pollini; and Virgin Classics, Chopin played by Piotr Anderszewski. The quotation from Brien Friel is taken from *Encore* program notes, November 2010, page 10.

Definitions of musical terms were taken from *The Oxford Companion to Music*, 2002.

"Solstice": The Harz is a range of low mountains in central Germany.

"Anne": I wrote this poem after reading Melissa Müller's *Anne Frank*.

"Beech": Caspar David Friedrich's painting, *Kreidefelsen auf Rügen* (Chalk Cliffs on Rügen), 1818, is perhaps his best known. Königstuhl is the place on the island of Rügen depicted in the painting.

"Gerüche": On February 13, 1945, allied bombers dropped firebombs on the civilian population of Dresden, causing two major firestorms and killing at least 35,000 civilians (and maybe as many as 135,000). The damage is sometimes compared to that of the atomic bombs dropped on Japan. Dresden had no military targets; the bombing is often seen as an act of revenge for the Nazi bombing of the medieval cathedral in Coventry, England.

"Armor" is freely imagined from fragments of a story I heard.

"In the Fields": The German word *Raps* rhymes with the English, *crops*. Contemporary incidents in the poem are freely imagined from story fragments.

"Finding the Poem": The quoted phrase was written by Tom Jay.

About the Author

Alice Derry is the author of four full collections of poetry. As manuscript, *Tremolo* was awarded a Washington State GAP grant from Artist Trust in 2011. *Strangers to Their Courage* (Louisiana State University Press, 2001) was a finalist for the 2002 Washington Book Award. Li-Young Lee writes of *Strangers*: "This book . . . asks us to surrender our simplistic ideas about race and prejudice, memory and forgetfulness, and begin to uncover a new paradigm for 'human.'" *Stages of Twilight* (Breitenbush, 1986) won the King County Publication Award, chosen by Raymond Carver. *Clearwater* appeared from Blue Begonia Press in 1997. Derry has three chapbooks: *Getting Used to the Body* (Sagittarius Press, 1989), *Not As You Once Imagined* (Trask House, 1993), and translations from the German poet Rainer Rilke (Pleasure Boat Studio, 2002). Derry's M.F.A. is from Goddard College (now Warren Wilson). After twenty-nine years teaching English and German at Peninsula College in Port Angeles on Washington's Olympic Peninsula, she retired in June, 2009. She was a major force in conceiving and directing the college's Foothills Writers' Series from 1980 to 2009.